Reedbed Diaspora

DEAR
AISHA

MAY ALLAH BLESS
YOU

ALWAYS +
ALL WAYS!,

S BLUZ

"My God, you have commanded me to return to created things, so return me to them with the raiment of lights and the guidance of inner vision, so that I may return from them to you just as I entered you from them."

– Ibn Ata'illah

"O God, if the night of separation is dark, we still rejoice, for the morning of union is near."

– Kwaja Abdullah Ansari

"Thus as we talked and yearned after eternal life,

we touched it for an instant with the whole force of our hearts.

We said, then, if the tumult of the flesh were hushed;

hushed these shadows of earth, sea, and sky;

hushed the heavens and the soul itself,

so that it should pass beyond itself and not think of itself:

if all dreams were hushed and all sensuous revelations,

and every tongue and every symbol;

if all that comes and goes were hushed...

turning their ear to Him who made them,

and that He alone spoke, not by them, but for Himself...

suppose we heard Him without any intermediary at all...

might not eternal life be like this moment of comprehension."

– Abd al-Rahman Jami

Listen to the reed how it tells a tale, bewailing separation's pain—

Saying, "Ever since I was parted from the reedbed, my cries have caused men and women to yearn.

Bring me a breast shattered by severance, (only to such a one) may I unfold the pain of love-desire.

Every one found far from his source yearns to return the moment of union.

In every circle I uttered my wailing notes; I was present with the saddest and the joyous just the same.

Everyone befriended me according to his own opinion; none sought out my secrets from within me.

My secret is not far from my lament, but ear and eye lack the light (that casts this vision).

Body is not veiled from soul, nor soul from body, yet none has permission to see the soul."

This sound of the reed is fire not breath; whoso hath not this fire, may he be naught.

'Tis the fire of Love that is in the reed, tis the fervor of Love that is in the wine.

The reed is the comrade of every one parted from a friend; its cries pierced our hearts.'

Who ever witnessed a poison and an antidote like the reed? Whoever saw a confidant and a longing lover like the reed?

– Mevlana Jalaludin Rumi

Reedbed Diaspora

Baraka Blue

barakablue

Dhikr Wagon Books

Oakland, CA

Dhikr Wagon Books
Published by Dhikr Wagon Publishing House

1919 Market Street, Suite 101
Oakland, CA 94607

Dhikr Wagon Publications: March 2013
ISBN: 978-1-300-91242-2
To contact Baraka Blue please email: barakablue@gmail.com
Printed in The United States of America

table of contents

introduction

These poems were written in the breaths since *Disembodied Kneelings* was published in 2010. Since then the words contained in those pages have traveled to every corner of the globe (sometimes with my accompaniment embodied and sometimes without). I have been honored and humbled to share them with friends and strangers and strangers turned friends. Along the way new inspirations surfaced and these poems are the result of a few that made their way into written form.

You will notice the poems are grouped in couples that follow a meditational theme presented in the form, "she said….." The *she said's* are themselves short poems, or mantras, koans, lessons, or wisdoms that have been attempting to realize themselves within me.

I wish not to color the readers' experience of these poems by offering much introduction but I did want to explain why I chose the title *Reedbed Diaspora*. The title of this book is drawn from the opening lines of Rumi's *Masnavi*, quoted above, in which he urges us to, "listen to the reed how it tells a tale." The reed flute, or *ney* as it is called in Arabic and Farsi, is an instrument that accompanied the drum in the gatherings of remembrance and invocation that Rumi held with his disciples. The *ney* is known for its beautiful yet melancholy notes. Anyone who has heard it can attest to its eerie broken-hearted cry. From the Quranic perspective, everything in creation is a sign drawing us back to the Creator. The *ney* is crying, Rumi tells us, because it was cut from its original home in the river bed. Cut from the reed bed, carted off and carved into an instrument, the reed flute was brought to the gathering of dervishes and given breath. When blown into it comes to life and cries, uttering its wailing notes in pure yearning for its original source—the reedbed. This cry is not only painful sadness; it is also intensely beautiful.

As with all stories in the Masnavi, the reader is supposed to understand that the characters are not outside him or herself. In this case, the reed flute represents the human being. We were cut from the primordial spiritual realm, from communion with our Source in the river of pure peace, light, and gnosis. Then given form, carved and blown into. In the Quranic narrative the breath of the Source of Mercy (*nafas ar-Rahman*) is blown into Adam, the primordial human. This breath gives him life, for it is his spirit and the seat of his consciousness. Adam, and all descendents who would follow him, after a time before time in the divine presence, witnessing and communing with the Ultimate Reality, were then brought out of this state, separated from this riverbed and placed in the here-below. We have come to this realm—according to the Sufis—to witness, remember and awaken to our original state of divine presence. This is the purpose of life and the reason for religion, revelation, and the spiritual path. The *ney* then, is an allegory of the human condition. Each human being is singing the song of their desire for reunion with their divine source, their primordial homeland. No matter how sad, beautiful, or cacophonic our songs have become, we are ultimately playing out this central impulse, whether we realize it or not. This world is the realm of separation. Yet separation from the eternally present is only a veil, a veil that is very real for those behind it. The *ney* is crying in beautifully painful nostalgia for its origin. And if we are listening closely we will find in its notes a means of return. For we are the Reedbed Diaspora.

she said,

live this dream
like you are awake
and if you are not awake
know the Awake
is watching
you dream

one voice

Imam Haddad and Black Elk speak
with the same voice
when will you see
that all language is symbol
all letters are signs

idols of clay and water
but the spirit resides

read between the lines
read beyond between
read behind

read within
don't just read the skin
read into her eyes
and realize that you
are kin

your sister it was
who gave birth to you

your mother it was

who nurtured you

your father it was
who searched for you

when you were lost
and tossed into the waves
of what was worst for you

but when they messaged in a bottle
you uncorked and you swallowed
each letter ever written
upon the scrolls of old
and hallowed
be thy names
arranged inside the microcosm's marrow
the way to follow the path
the ancestors have modeled

and it was their eyes
staring back at you

through
yesterday's tomorrow

as the night sky spoke

a silent language
that we all know

and you remember you were always literate
in that glittering sun script

the vision realer
than reality
as celestial scales unveiled
their symmetry

and now the speech was close and clear
like thunder whispering in your ear

with a harmony so precise
it let escape no noise

and Imam Haddad and Black Elk spoke
with the same voice

ancestors' angels sung the chorus
that went, "*you,*
you have no choice
you've been chosen
remember why you've come
if you forget you've been destroyed"

it was gorgeous in its awesomeness
beyond a pleasure or a pain
it was all our souls together
bearing witness on that plain

a million precious reed flutes
carefully carved
and given breath

a single truth on fire
in each and every breast

it's Lao Tzu and Gautama
Moses, Jesus, all the rest
it's the light of Muhammad
coursing through your very flesh

it's the counsel of elders
sages, seers, and of saints
it's all your ancestral mothers
saying, "*hush child*
it is late"

it's the glorious copulation
of a joined free will and fate
the completion of the circle

it's Adam's reawakened state

to realize all creation
all his children's stories great
was all simply a vision
right before he almost ate

as all one formless body
it bows and it prostrates

"*am I not your Lord?*"
answering, "*Yes*"
one voice quaked.

timeline brushstrokes

there are so many nows
wrapped up   in your face wrinkles
      so many intensities
so many becomings
innumerable minuscule   now-beads   strung
together bejewel   your complexion
you are   highly decorated   with scars

     riverbed cheeks know
               periodic floods
mote-trenches around your eye castles
guard   what sieges keep   trapped   inside
pathways to pleasure and power
layer like   rose blossom   laugh lines

your   sweet scented   mouth
     now   usually   latched shut
on special occasions heralds trumpet-announce
as you pronounce but
the   long oratories   of before   have mostly been
               renounced

have you ever been   in   love ?   she asked

how could I ever get out   ?

there's something   tangible   in your   silence
something   violent
 in your   breaths
there's a   distance   in your   discourse
a solemn   in your   steps
there's a   poverty   in your   poetry

a   painfulness   in your
party
line
it could almost be   haunting

          almost be   divine
it could
          almost be   humorous

          almost be   like dying

it could
          almost   ruin   everything
almost
          make it   all   fine
it could
          almost be   nothingness

it is oh such a   fine line

if you look close enough   stages are   discernible
a timeline is etched   from fetus to present
    possibly past that
    most likely before
there's war and   there's wisdom
the poor   and the prisons
and more
there's rest and   there's rhythm
violence   and   victim
there's victory
              and   vision

there's death
              and   destruction
there's dance
              and   discussion
there's sex
              and   there's sunsets
there's silence
              and   sound
there's   moments of madness
there's the piercing   profound
mistakes
              and   misjudgment

burnt bridges
      and   hearts
sh a tt er ed to p iece s
there's such light
      and   such dark
each one   is a painter
each moment   making a mark
when you die   you step   out

     of the painting

and you look at your art

she said,

I never forgot

who you always were

after the rain

how can I write to this?
how can I
       not

it is the purest
       most sacred
sadness
       ever expressed

the sound of tears forming
       behind the eyelids
         of unborn children
this loneliness woven
       into pregnant mother's womb rhythms
all of us prenatally baptized
           in blue
don't you?
       don't you?
         don't you remember?
I know you do
       its autumn in New York
       all over again
Sarah Vaughn opens her mouth and a long

                necked swan bows
graceful   and shy
    and after the rain
we sat silent and our souls slow danced
                        until they dried
melancholy memories
            of something I can't quite
grasp
        hold
                        of
I stopped trying and let it become me
        and it always was
                                what it really did was remind me
of what it was
            that I can't remember
                    that I always was

there are words for things
        in   time   and   space
there are words   for thoughts
            words   for feelings
there are words   for words
        there are no words
for   this
            nor will there ever   be
hopeless   as these   poet's breaths

may   sound
in charging
            fearlessly   into a sea
        of enemy soldiers
    the greatest victory   is gained
except
                    this is   no enemy
for I am victorious when   it has been given victory
                            over me
        when I let it become   me
                let it become
                    become
                    be

in this moment
            any other sound   would be profanity
    all other articulations blasphemy
                            this language
allowed solely because it exists only
to make sense
                of you
how senseless

                                        absurd
yet   it is also

the only endeavor
　　that has ever been worth undertaking

look how you manifest　　　　your beauty
　　and majesty
　　　　　　　　　　at once
all wrapped up
　　　　in each other　　　　indistinguishably
　　　　　you are so beautiful　　it is crippling
so unbridled　　it is comforting

at once
　　　　I am　　ashamed　　　of　these　　　　words
　　　and inspired　　to express　　this
wave　　from ocean floor　　　this shoreless sunset reflection
　　　　this darkless light
　　　　　　　　　　　this starless　night
this veil that parts　　for hearts
　　but not　　for sight
don't confuse me
　　　everything I say is wrong
right can't be said　　or read　　　or carved
　　no art　　　even a spark　　　ignites
of this　　fire
　　　　enveloping a heart
　in　flight

3rd & James [lost angels]

you make me want to write wings   on lost angels
gutter griots
stutter   eloquent   incoherence
slave kings dig
                    through dumpsters   for scraps
of lost nobility
grown orphans   soul sting
of abandoned empathy
every single cosmic energy descends
on the flame pulled into a crack pipe

descendents of stolen peace pipes
shattered treaty sincerities   ask   *what's honesty*
wounded warriors   rain dance   in tranquility famines
the cipher of war transgenerational
    smoke signals atop
sacred plains imprisoned
concrete suffocated and
barbed wired

you make me want to extend everything   on tongue tips
into unstained glass windows
    to soul seats

of unborn infants
with genetic codes predestined
   to death and destruction
   disdain and despair

you make me want to pierce prose   with prayer

inverted innocence
scribbled on loose leaf sheets and taped
to the collective refrigerator
daughters of grandmother spirits sip
spirits and unveil their vessels
to extent the essence within is
veiled from self perception

[exit stage left]

appearance of presence surface
at best
she's running with the pack   [pounding hooves
panting breath]
destination: as far as possible from self
souls threadbare
reverse exorcisms are coping mechanisms
when your dream catcher has seen too many nightmares
eyes vacant

the sacred in her veiled
from wolf eyes
who gaze upon her thighs
naked

I'd
hit
that

exhaled liquor lipped
by a warrior's son with heels clay caked red
who tracked the living to give life
to dead siblings
who forked tongue led
slipperly into the lions den transatlantic
feeding the furnace ambitions
of the passionate
slaves to the basest appetence
look how it gives birth
to itself
never satiated
ever perpetuating its avarice

brought back to the block I stand on
by the ring of an ambulance
as lusts birth more

blank slates to write

violence on

it's dark and dawn

seekers have all

but gone

I fear

it's too late for those

who've stumbled within earshot

of the siren's song

she said,

your name
     on my tongue
     humbles honey

all that you pour

I want to open you   once-and-for-all

pearl your unseen   bottle your weathered sea glass

in my throat

you Khidr my heart-vessel

Hu impregnated your Maryam saliva and Jesus heals my leper'd heart
in your

psalm melodies

I hummingbird in your throat nectar

I cut myself in your exhalations' Joseph's faces

men are killed for speaking this tongue

but silence is endless death

all these tears form the ocean necessary to sail this messaged bottle

        to your inner island

other cheeks are   deserts   of despair

these rivers float hope and open mid air

a thousand winged reed flutes   stork drop

primordially conceived prayers

penetrating your veiled layer

and

       and

            and

   all these words are cheap liquor

your eyes the only wine that pours

                                        purity
it is here with turbaned heart nobility
I am

                  poor
I must return to preparing my cup
for all that you   pour

growing in

there's a

       growing in

              that's like winter

there's a

       growing in   that sheds light

a light behind your breath that casts itself out

there's a

       growing in   like roots

taking   deeper   hold

       a growing in like blown glass

changing form

everything grows up

not everything   grows in

there's a

       growing in that makes   everything

more

      [and less]

              real

a growing in that makes the little   large
the unnoticed   gesture   glow
the unmimicked movement matter more   than all the glittering
trophies ribboned

there's a
        growing in   that fills   emptiness
that makes   moments never pass   too   slow

each one a bead moved   across a string   by a transcendent
hand
each holy rosary   rosy cheeked beloved   opening
offering
          its graceful fragrance   in proportion   to what you
forfeit
of yourself   unto it   fully
but you can offer   only
the amount   you have   grown   in

there is a
        growing in
                that is most tangible
                                mornings

a tangerine   unpeeled center   growing
a seed unseen   sowing itself   into your being   a growing
into the soil of your soul ceiling

                    a seedling piercing your heart earth

as if giving birth   in   slow   motion

petals unfolding fully   into knowing

feeling   your focus

peel   through   layers   formerly associated   with selfhood

nearing the locus

kneeling

                    exposing yourself to the healing   hypnosis

of the   Real

                    approaching the oceans

of shorelessness

            hearing the horses hooves   pounding   closer and
closer

in   the   mirror

from   clearing   its face   with the moistness

of tongue   from the names

                till they rain

                        down   on your heart   in a million   voices

as if

        hummed. [*hamd. hamd.*]

    prayers woven

of pure harmonic tapestry

as the inner witness

that has grown in   sown

and stitched   in to the seat   of your consciousness
follows this   stream   up   its   vibratory   current
like   lotus flower   floating   your offering

                                  to river's source

only to find that   the source   of these infinite voices   is one
throat

       one   breath
from one   breast
       one   *"be!"*
       one   *"alestu'*

                 bi-

Rabbi kum"

till you have

      but become

      one   *"Yes."*

there is a

         growing in

that makes a   silent   moment

                          before dawn

like that

that makes the world less   solid   but more   vivid

that makes you   entirely present   yet indescribably
distant

there is a

        growing in   that imprints   its seal   on the wax   of
your being

and delivers you   out

and back into   existence

        each instant

there is

      a growing in   by which you   no longer see

but you witness

she said,

if
  you can't see God
                        [in everything]
  you can't see God

heart mirror

no
I don't want to see your thong
I want to see the sun

               set   in your throat
and the winged moment   netted   in your eye glitter
and the exposition of your tongueless yearning   refracted
off an   alley-brick-wall
in a   time   suspended
urban wilderness
and God

            reflected

                     in your   heart mirror
when I stare   into you   to see myself

and Jesus

       Christ's   footprints   in your saliva

pour me the memories   that most scalded
                  the   roof   of your
                     mouth
let's make this about above   desire
let's make silence

less   awkward

          than speech

let's make mournings   the most sacred   part of our day

          again

[I swear to God]

I want to love you
as powerfully as one
who loves nothing but God
loves everything

I want to be your   Zen *koan* unlocked

          your   Quranic verse unveiled

the dim   rusty   street   light   above

          the   sh a tt er ed   piece s

               of your   lost
forever

these words bow   in shame

at their utter incapacity
to   articulate   that which   inspires   their   existence
like believers tear fully acknowledging

               their deficiency in

gratitude and submission   to their infinitely merciful and
bountiful source-sustenance

you breathed my existence out of nothingness
no other risk is rational
but spending all my *risq* to get back to you
my reason is your creation
or I was created for no reason
no response but remembrance
is reasonable
all other thoughts are treason

I've faced the fact that
to face any other face is
vanity
for *all is perishing except your countenance*
all other pronouncements are profanity
I want to chase you
into a field of primordial openings
that is all

gasoline puddles

I.

the first and the last
the sacred and the profane
the beautiful and the grotesque   meshed
into your flesh

                          woven
technicolor dream coat painted
on that which gathered
upon what was perpetrated   on our mother's skin
tarred and feathered
wings oil slicked
the blood of ancestral life forms stolen
        to fuel cement sanctuaries of sacrilege
        shrines to the bottom line
your baptism in electric wine   the psychedelic blood
of metallic saviors
robotic vampires   erratic behavior
vines of pollution wind
                        slithering
into every   crevice   of your mind
        constricting slowly
severing   every memory of the time before

time

distraction
                              disease
            discord
                                        chaotic action
cacophonous   constant   motion
        ecstatic passions
moments frozen
                              in violent corruption
pollution   corrosion   explosion

II.

the purest life elixir
clarity   quenching
flowing oasis energy
sentient being
precious symbol
of submission
yin of yearning
womb rhythms you are
that which knew Jesus' footprints
Muhammad's fingertips
Moses' staff splits

Hagar's heal
Abraham's lips
the cure and the cleansing
the source of all return
the primordial essence
the thirst that was birthed from separation
you quenched it
the depths is you
the riverbed you wept it
rain dance
growth
renewal
replenish
replenish
replenish
the essence
the essence
the essence

III.

you met
and the celestial spark locus expression
birth of direction
	from the placeless center spawned

the spectrum

from the bosom of the colorless

breathless mother of

presence

"*be!*" and we were

present

and the slave gave birth

to her master

and the now gave birth

to hereafter

and your pain gave birth

to your laughter

in puddles on your cheeks

tears rushing to the lowest

point in the street

and the puddles on your cheeks

where rivers run

and blood

sweat and tears   meet

exploding into the spectrum   that your soul selects from

celestial palates

making beauty

out of the hate they gave you

spirit so subtle

making love

in the ruins, and dancing

in the rubble

all while staring at

your reflection in a gasoline puddle

she said,

no created speech
            is more eloquent
than the tongue-state   of the heart
yearning to disappear

in God

light language

since you left
I've been cheating
with language

the way she undresses me
sits gentle on my tongue
draws ecstasies out of me
invites   to expose her
exchange her essence
for mine

I can't deny
our love
her breaths consume me

still

I'd renounce her lips forever
        if that would return you

despite infidelities' cloak
I cannot say I've been seeing someone else

you see

      I only love her   because   she

sometimes
          [when
               the light
                   hits
                        her right]
       reminds me

             of you

shoreless

                          behind
that random richness
beneath
that beautiful bizarre
there is a knower   and an unknown
there is a baby girl
                    and a showcase of stardust melody
there is a dewdrop sweetness
                    under
                    your tongue

that tongue is not
in   your   mouth
that tongue is a   door   to a tongueless universe
that is the door   I want   to kiss
                                    open
lovers lock lips
to unlock   this
        only   lovers

she said

step off   the tip   of my tongue into this universe

suspended here   *in your opening*

forgive me for being so   *forward*
but all other
                        words are backwards
and even these   mere   diving boards

                                        shoreless ocean   beneath
you

she said,

everything is
touching everything
else

through a window

this art is passionate   conversation
across pavement's breast
                    through windows paned

you can't tell if it's laughter
        or anger

if it's love
        or it's hatred

all you know   is you're captured
            captivated

you just stand there   gaping
and gasping
                        and waiting
it's madness and mayhem
it's sane and it's safe

but
it's danger and   pain
                in prostration

it's raw   inspiration

       perspiration in prayer
is that despair
in his face   or jubilation
is she crying or shaking
are they fighting or making
              love
are they dying or procreating

are they singing or screaming
are they coming or leaving
are they humming or breathing

                    numbing   or   feeling

are they leading   each other   astray
and   deceiving
are they cheating
or treating   each other
        to a wonderful   evening

you are my favorite poem

you are my favorite poem
the way you write yourself into me
lips bleeding backwards

your fragility is dominating
your moans crushing
you blush violently

I am a soldier in a far off land
whose last source of hope
is dying into you

[in   to you]
there is depth so dark
it is blinding
a moon so bright
there's been no sighting
a pain so intense
it's ecstasy
a joy so sharp
it's frightening
it's from there
that you were written

it's from there
that you
are writing

she said,

you are a master
only to the extent
you have become a slave

rain

and wetness pervades
it slips into every crevice of the vessel   seeking the resistanceless
point
absolute submission prostrates

        forever
until quieted to

           rest
by an embrace
  honoring the shape of its mold
ever content where
 directed
be it fountain   pot or sewer

          drain

like a sage in ecstatic prayer

             it seeks the deepest depth
content with every form
perfectly   patient   in every

           space
it's made   to rest
yet unattached   to every dam   or quarried well
perfectly present   with every opening   deeper
whether trickling   drip   or majestic

                                falls

until becoming absent to itself   in ascension to the *barzaq*

then   regaining individuation & falling

                         swiftly   to

the terrestrial realm

only to embrace submission's ever increase once again

maybe months   maybe years

perhaps in gushing floods or

meandering streams

often assuming all these forms

                       and more

in a single lifetime

  somehow ever patient   [yet ever focused]

                          on its goal

it is there

            on the day

maybe distant   maybe soon

when the running and the crashing

the damming and the falling

the raging rapids and the

silent pools

the powerful force   and the gentle   mist

all reach their culmination in the destiny which every
                              drop   forever
yearns
passing away   through the river's threshold mouth
merging once and for all
with the knowing ocean
finally home
in shoreless sea

daughter of the moment

she laid there in her bed
and she slightly swayed her head
whispering beneath her breath
couldn't make out what she said

she laid there in her bed
and she gently swayed her head
watering beneath my skin
the visions that she bled

I couldn't escape her sadness
could not escape her charm
I couldn't escape her blessing
could not escape her harm

I was cast into the depths of the oceans
in her eyes
swept into the storms that raged
intently in her sighs

she laid there in her bed
she slightly swayed her head
whispering beneath her breath

I couldn't make out what she said

she laid there in her bed
and gently swayed her head
I almost spoke to ask her
but I closed my eyes instead

and focused on the words
her heart was beating
in that moment
I saw that all that was
was fleeting

as I felt her head a'sway
I knew all that is
must pass away
and felt a wilting like a rose
in changing seasons

my flesh melting from my bones
I felt so all alone

looked down upon my hands in fear
a'reeling

she looked into my eyes
I felt her gaze set deep inside
and knew she knew just what it was
that I was feeling

as I sat beside her bed
tears rolling down my head
there I was all broken down
and kneeling

as one rolled off my lip
the melon moonlight hit
and all at once I felt her
felt her healing

she said,
I am but a daughter of the moment
the moment is a drop within the ocean
you must dive until you're lost to every notion
of separation from the current's motion

I am but the daughter of the moment
and you are just a drop within the ocean
she plunged me in the waves of her devotion
until I had but become the current's motion

she laid there in her bed
and she gently swayed her head
I almost spoke to ask her
but I closed my eyes instead

she laid there in her bed
and she gently swayed her head
watering beneath my skin
the visions that she bled

she said,

you can never escape

slavery

but you can   choose

your master

beloved

Can you imagine one who was the gentlest of men
while being the most brave and just of all who've been
one who conquered all desires of self that make men weak
who granted all who asked him precisely what they seek

whom only jewels poured out his mouth whenever he would speak
who was the gem amongst the stones of men who shined unique
a selflessness and generosity that some would say
was merely myth until they'd seen the lovers of his way

who used to mend his sandals, used to patch his clothes
who used to serve his family whenever he was home
who had a noble shyness, not gazing long upon a face
who honored all he ever met, be he king or be he slave

who always felt himself at home the most among the poor
who never angered for himself but only for his Lord
always just, always truthful, conscious of the One
even if it brought discomfort to himself and those he loved

a satiated stomach his whole life was rarely felt
not due to poverty but preference of others to himself
who knew the time of day by sun, the direction by the stars

who'd walk amongst his enemies without a single guard

devoid of any lower self, just humble and serene
eloquent but not verbose, just precisely what he means

whom all within his company felt light and sacred cheer
whom there was not a thing within creation that he feared

who loved to play with children and run races with his wives
who'd join the festivities and honor customs of all tribes
when people yelled and lost their cool around him he was calm
who asked forgiveness for his enemies even as they did him wrong

who kept a goat he'd milk himself for people in his house
whose wives when asked about him said, *"he was the perfect spouse"*
who never looked down on a pauper or flattered once a prince
who called every soul unto the One without even a flinch

every single gorgeous trait of character he had
of noble lineage yet he was the orphan of his clan
one imbued with wisdom and piercing inner sight
yet he was the unlettered one who'd neither read nor write

all knowledge and trait of character unflawed
were placed inside his very being directly by Allah
the way to salvation and triumph after death

to detachment and joy in life with each and every breath

to walk the righteous path and never falter come what may
and may Allah give us success in following his way
they call him al-Amin, the trustworthy, the honest
and I call him beloved, my master Muhammad

(May the Most High shower infinite peace and eternal blessings upon him)

in awe

my face is honest with yours
that music of eye glitter is more valuable
than every delicate rareness
you can trust me
in this moment
a word has never been wagered weightier
I'll wait here
in your pendulum
token of appreciation
your lips make me in awe of God

she said,

don't assume the map
 is wrong
because some people with the map
are lost

sub-stance

memory lane broken lampshade
[in a circle]
tell everyone what you're scared of

what do you associate with being satiated?

rebellion is right
she said
but is more often destructive than constructive
de-con-struct sub-stance
what supplies you with sustenance?
[breakdance]
what stance did you come out of the womb in?
prostrate to tomb music
[subs rattle trunk]

what are we supposed to remember again

let's stand at this crossroads
and laugh at our death
and cry at our laughing
and yell at our silence
and be moved by our stillness
and be safe from our viciousness
and believe in believing
and knowing the knower
and now

and different levels
[*oh, you still on that?*]
I'm still on this

old blocks
new faces

twothousandandnow
still calling on the Great Spirit in Cherokee
and *'Arabee.*
singing songs of reverse frontier marching
facing backwards
[it's forwards]

to look ahead

[prostrate]

what are we supposed to remember again?

can't see past my *me*-ness

this after a morning of sadness

a mourning

she said,

no one
is self made

every one
is Self made

akbar

it is greater than anything you could ever think *it* is
it is greater than anything I could   ever say *it* is

the expanse of the universe   dipped   in harmonic oneness
geometric patterns   woven into and out of existence
have warmth   and light   and texture
and tongues
              to sing you their secrets   in the   language beyond
until you weep of angelic procession
the tears   transform   crystalline   psychedelic
      on your cheek
each one attended by innumerable light beings
each being blowing trumpets made from colors   supraspectrum
you develop new eyes   to see them
      your vision unfolds   kaleidoscopic
each unfolding able to absorb more beyond light color
and the   depth   expanding   with every unfolding
         never stagnant   or exhausted

[*it* is greater than that]

'stagnant' or 'exhausted' are concepts

                                        that have never penetrated
this realm
this realm is
an ageless oasis   opening   into awnings   above oracles
                who only point   in ecstasy
                        to a pointless center
lotus seed soaked in   *OM* and *HU*
this oil that lights soul soil

a wick   bears witness   to its own nonexistence   and women whisper
of incandescent imprints   on your mirror's image
infants whimper   as the wind whisks this   all away
  into a sand grain   that lifts its   head and bows before
merging   into a desert   of its siblings

each sand grain similar
yet original and indescribably different

[*it* is greater than all that]

each desert rests   inside a droplet
            each droplet   inside an ocean
            and each ocean inside a breath
                                a breath   inside your breast
            as you exhale your first: "*Yes.*

Indeed you are my Lord,

my Lord,

indeed I am your breath."

[and yet
it is still greater]

that may be getting closer
[but only] closer in the way   yesterday   was closer to   infinity
    than the day before it
see this language-game is for fools   and if you are listening
      you are less reputable   than the speaker

[but if you put your ear closer to the speaker
you may hear her say]

there is no speaker

but the exhale

no listener

but the inhale

there is no you   or   me

or desert   or   sea

or she   or

     [or...

       or...]

there is no   there

no   is

no   no

there is   nothing   being   spoken

there is   no speaker   to say it

there is   nothingness

there is   no nothingness

there is   nothing-less

it is so much greater that   it is even less than this

there is no sanity   but being

                              in-sanity

  there is no word   that is not   profanity

there is no saint   that   sees himself

there is   no self   that is not vanity

I've fallen   into the   pit   I've dug to catch you

and as great as this   bottomless pit is

   it   is   greater   than that too

tattoo

when a tattoo isn't deep enough

and being shallow may never go out of style
but when it finally sinks in
                most regret it

she inks flaming hearts and virgin Marys on my ethereal body
            with sharpened tongue tip

            mother and lover
            dead homie and brother
                                    … brother sit still
                                    it only hurts for a second
but the pain will never wear off

explain to me what forever means
can I take it with me?

she screamed *look at me* then hid
the *me* behind *look*

and I would know you better if I never saw

but all the memorable moments are mapped here
    this one was my first love   that one my greatest fear
        my darkest hour
        my block-name
        my strength   my search for meaning
        my god
until I ran out of space to say what I
wasn't saying
until I no longer noticed myself   in the images I'd drawn to
catch you

and found my own skin foreign

she tattooed her spirit to my tongue
and made me tell her what I really mean

and she finally witnessed   what she'd been hiding
behind those words all along
and I finally witnessed   I'd been hiding
behind my words all along